In memory of my grandmothers, Geraldine and Vita

TABLE OF CONTENTS

III

PROLOGUE

You spoke of the followers of a mathematician who drew
from his example the promise of a second life. Pythagoras
lived as Pythagoras. And, having chosen the weapon
of an ancestor from a pile, he lived again, or that earlier hero
whose weapon he had chosen lived a second life in him.
Now that it is sure the both of them are dead, your take
on the old question stings us iron and fresh: *what good
does it do the hero to have stood for something once?*
The sea eats the captain and his crew. The aged still tear
at the bright youths and those in their prime on their way
to the underworld, tumbling down as if they, too,
were young again. Nobody escapes the sport of the old gods
or the shame of the new Christ, cold in his chiefly literal state.
Stay with us. We will need you soon enough. Stay to confound

what might be termed the second life of Edward Teller,
our father of the H-bomb, what with the ethos he delivered once,
his theme, reprised by the stiffs come to trade upon his take
on the human condition: the heart's essential weakness,
the self-serving nature of humankind, our vision, base,
not visionary, caught wittling down the truth. That Teller
was no Pythagoras, in truth, come, tell us. Come sink these stiffs
already bidding in his name for a licence to spread a sea of mirrors
into space so as to make the sunlight flicker and to cool
what they have frequently termed this sunken earth. They will ask
to dust the stratosphere, too, with haze enough to reproduce
what Vesuvius and Mount St. Helens threw upon the day-
light once. They will ask to engineer a thick albeit
temporary age of winter, to put an end to the warmth

we forced upon the atmosphere and in upon ourselves
in this (and it is almost fair) our bent for self-indulgence.
Set us right again. Ask this group the old question,

and in an even sharper strain of certitude, *what good
does it do you now that you are dead* (though they
remain, for all intents and purposes, among the living)
*to have treated our predicament from the tips and not
the roots?* Ask them, *what good,* not to confirm in us
our primal lethargy but to make it plain – the most of us
would choose, on behalf of our two hemispheres and their
surrounding gases, to go without our deeper wants
and most of our possessions, with little grief, and long
before we make our way to Proserpina, swung at and torn
by the aged and the youths enticed or bidden there.

I

SURVEILLANCE

But Light a newer Wilderness
My Wilderness has made –
        – Emily Dickinson

One of the neighbourhood dogs, we imagined,
was sure to emerge from the woods with a rabbit
or a squirrel, or some other prize, dangling, bloody,
from its mouth. But nothing would come out.
And the threshing, the trampling in the woods
behind our house would not dull down.

So we came to divine them, the surveyors,
by the sounds they made with their instruments,
the retractable tape lines scuttling and riffing
along the way, the pick and sledge keening those
four metal posts into the earth, the fluoro-paint
flushing against a defensive row of ferns
or whipping bold stripes across the fisticuffed
knots of the scrub oaks.

                        And we supposed
that though we were separated from those men
by porch screens, a sloping yard, the creek bed
at its foot, and the few rows of trees that were part
of our land, what we owned – and even considering
the layer of kudzu that covered everything, some said
the whole state – the men lay hidden more for what
was behind them than the clutter between us, a miles-
thick backdrop of trees and ferns so green it was ash.

How their measurements collected and ventured out
over the vines that clung to the woods and stalked up
our hill. As they raffled off their inches and feet

and translated them into metres, how those thrown
voices beat into us there, high on the screened-in porch,
the volume only increased for the canopied distance
the utterances travelled.

                              And then their total exposure.
How one of the men bent over his measuring tool,
and how we spotted him, his orange helmet catching
a slant of light that stripped through the kudzu, flashing
it back out at us. We witnessed the outline of a man
coining forward from the woods, an x-ray of a body
doubled over a measuring tool, hurtling through
the greenery in one illuminating flash.

                                        A full
minute later, as if in response, the second project-man,
spaced a quarter-mile or so away from the first, caught
another shaft of sun on his hard hat, sending himself,
or the image of his whole body, careening out from the thick.
One body, then the other. I could not help but think
of a line between the two, the completion of a project.

You said it was a signature, that bright light,
or the bodies, pausing the way they did, repeating –
a sign, you said, but only a detail of what it would be like
after the clearing, when the thick behind our own
clutter of woods got removed. Remember, you spoke
with such gravity. Our woods would prove nothing
but a wind barrier then, some thin relief.

                                   And especially
at sunset, the light would pervade the new clearing,
seeping through our trees, willing us no peace

of darkness and no shade, that light would aggravate
and undo, that congealed yellow glut, the effect
(you had to build upon the most immediate image)
of the sun's taking charge of a thousand hard
hats on a thousand men, bent over in surveillance.

MINERS' HOUSES

This town once had its inhabitants.
Bitten by the coal and gone under
for it, they lit-tindered the bases
of the hills as they disappeared.
If you were a tourist you would take
a tethered swing or a freight
elevator between the heaps
and try to study how they broke,
like those eighteenth-century
English travellers who kept
to their own nation for the sake
of economy, tackling the peaks,
writing their friends direct
from the man-made grottoes,
quoting Milton as they shuttled
down into the quarries for a view.

Risen again, you would find
all the two-storey houses high
in a rage for collecting, clapped
down over their catalogues
and books pierced with crickets
or the exoskeletons of southern
insects, their dust bins kept
brimming with the ends of linens
and newspaper clippings. A bird's nest,
or a bear's head levelled against
a few gallons of fixative, prepared
for the conclusion of its taxidermy –
almost all of the contents they
cater to and bless, these houses,
combustible, except for the array
of cast trilobites organized

on the side table, there, or the jar
of marbles just to the right
side of the period instruments
not yet strung or tuned.

This is an easier rage to divine.
The curtains all part slightly
at the sashes. And you can see that
as sure as the sky parts, pointing
its dove boulder down to oil them all,
these houses, in blue-backed
sheets of light, not one will stand
deprived of its possessions.

IN DEFENCE OF BURNING

Not much of a rite, Cassandra, holding
over the ovens, watching for her cut-outs
to seize above the coals, to spread out and to lick
into ships of ash (as if the paper, burning,
rose up like one of those women we have read
about, wild, in the ancient romances, tearing
at the unroped hair conversant with her cheek-
bones and her raw chest) at last sifting through
the errors between the coals, an unterrific
heated dust. Right, Cassandra, hedging, maybe,
or grinning a little at the utterances she weeds
from her sister's letters and family papers,
those privacies set aside to burn. Cassandra,
burning her clippings of all the insincere
and illegitimate issues, her sister's caricatures
of neighbours and no ones, her own scrawl
on the progress of a fever she watched shooting bull
red through the face of a woman at Lyme,
accounts of the accounting or the hairdresser's
bills – or better, Cassandra, well within her rights,
editing out and burning the serious confessions,
all the appalled relations of an esteem here,
a resemblance there, or a foreboding – evidence
that full well might have influenced even the murkiest
sense to try for something similar in the way
of a real attachment, or to stand down, surveying
a lean loss without that much affectation,

or to refuse, at last, and as a rule, to spend
any sentence of time converting a mean, more
beautiful man into an angel. To dull her scissors,
to let those sentences and subjects burn stands
hers in the right. Now who would go and regret
this burning for all it omits and withholds?

And how sore would you need to be to insist
in some kinetic, modern way that even if we cannot
play privy to this burnt out correspondence
between sisters, these pits and pats gone out, now,
and down with the kitchen scraps, that this act,
in and of itself, this event, as you might call it,
would have tickled or tainted the play of one
of the minor figures in what you must imagine, now,
as the scene, driving down to stroke us, too: as if
the local Mary would have glimpsed Cassandra
burning her sister's letters and instinctively passed
a tear as she passed by the side window; as if
the kitchen Jane would have made a lucky turn,
gotten herself into better circumstances, say,
a wholesome marriage, because she heard
an extra hiss or whistle in the cook's report
of delays with the dinner, heard that whistle
and changed her mind about things. What is it
that you have come to expect? That if the gardener,
bent over the thawed vegetable patch, caught
a glimpse of the kitchen fire, something new
or notable would have formed in him, in us,
and for posterity's sake? Nothing bloomed out
of fashion under the hands of the old haggard
who would not have watched a word start from one
blazing page and have thought to look affectionately

on the first greens or to make hybrids of the border's
standard rose. No glimpses over his shoulder and up
and through Cassandra, burning the letters.
No killing cuts in the wood of the lavender,
having lunged too far forward with the knife.

LULLABY

I cannot imagine you called to be a martyr.
I have seen too many pictures of those
famished things offering up images
and the implements of their own torture.
This saint, here, blindfolded, holding
her eyes in front of her in a coal iron.
That harried Veronica presenting a cloth
fresh-bled with the face of her victim Jesus.

I cannot see you as a botanist either. What
with everyone so acclimatized to the beautiful,
only the weeds with their enticing names
would interest the governors in their grants.
Sure, it might originate, your research,
from an urge to restore the more natural
charms, from a whole and hearty longing
(and I expect you will be set longing)
to eradicate diseases like tulip fire, to set
buds upon the blind daffodils, to force
the deadly nightshade from the ivy for now
and for good. But for you, for any of us,
despite the initial calling, there would be no
chance of being drawn back, in the end,
to a survey of the consistent fruiting
and flowering of oranges and hollyhocks.

No, do not go and be anything.
Just sit here shallowing and unbred.
In the old way, I am out to murder Vocation.

THE EARS OF KINGS

Within a living register, a collection of all the flora ever
     mentioned in the works of Shakespeare, a college garden,
     enclosed by hedges,
backed by a church, you caught the shadow of a bird skating
     forward from the leeks, and you told me, once again, how
     much you hate the starlings.
As if I had never heard it before, didn't know you despised the
     starlings or the man who, as you say, inflicted them on us all,
you called him out, *Eugene Schieffelin*, by his full name, as if
     you wanted to invoke his ghost or had caught him as a
     child in a lie or in some minor promiscuity
that might lead to something sinister in his adult life. You
     summoned him, *the drug manufacturer*, emphasizing the
     mischief
in his career as chemist or pharmacist in a backwards
     Victorian age, and I saw him there with us, if only for a
     moment, among the roses and medicinal herbs, talking of
     the starlings
and their potency, more of a quack than a boss man, waving
     jars of pills in the air around his head, *there's rue for you*, I
     thought he might have said.

Sinister enough, so the flight began. You related to me and to
     the bearded irises, withered then and drying,
how Schieffelin organized the introduction of all the non-
     native avian species ever mentioned in Shakespeare's
     plays. One evening in 1890 (you tossed them up
in the sky with your fists, a couple of birds) eighty starlings
     started from their cages and gathered in the open air
     above an amphitheatre in Central Park, winging wide and
     crowning
into forty pairs, couples on couples, the starlings keeping to
     their own race amidst the furious paddling of the thrushes

and finches and whatever other birds Shakespeare
happened to settle upon in the plays.
And as you settled into the story of their spreading, I saw the
starlings taking to the eaves of the Museum of Natural
History,
building their nests, their spotted feathers half red with labour.
And I managed to see them, too, as you described them in
their reaches,

only a few years after their initial release, flocked along the
Mississippi, catching discards from the riverboats before
any one of those kitchen scraps or soiled papers could strike
the water. You said *Schieffelin's Starlings* drove off native
species, the blue birds, woodpeckers, Carolina parakeets,
and I saw an individual starling cover over the blue
body of one of those blue birds and trample it to death, his
spots blurry furious, shunting whole corruption.
And your chorus – how the muscles in the jaws of the starlings
were engineered by some more vindictive God to open
rather than to close
as is the normal manner of birds, so that their songs, though
you had to call them startles, carried over and crooned at
least three times
louder than the calls of native species. With this I thought to
see a girl on her porch in Alaska, not more than nine,
forming the shadows of curse words
with her hands against the night sun because she was deafened
at some point earlier on, after being delivered into her
mother's arms, say,

or while sitting too long under the hemlock, deafened by the
starlings and all the mimic sounds of North America
they drew across her as they arrived, en masse, sometime in

the nineteen-seventies.
You went on about the starlings flooding our continent in only
        a few decades, grimacing *Eugene Schieffelin*,
and the starlings grunted his name, too, their wings raised up
        beside them and their bodies forward-facing, fucking
like humans in nests of their own guano, nests that lined the
        rafters of an Iqaluit storehouse and the power grids
        outside of Mexico City – all at once – I saw them massed
        in silver silos
hulking over the heaped grain. And the lights in a farmhouse
        and a city condominium shut off simultaneously because
        one starling got caught somewhere

in one sorry spot along this chain of being, starting a reaction.
        And in this international blackout I had concocted in and
        around your story, and
despite the extinguishing of all the man-made lights in the
        night sky, I could not even glimpse the moon or the
        satellites, because the starlings
spread out in a net, blocking all the sky imaginable with their
        bodies, their own starry spots reflecting nothing.
With all this, you struck, finally, upon your sternest warning.
        The point, you would say, of all this history was that we
        have been destroying
our environment, and that we had better consider things more
        seriously before planting more imported shrubs or sending
        French guinea fowls to our aunt Cecelies in Idaho.
Some warning, and, because of its general nature, strange. You
        must have known, for instance, that Schieffelin's
        initial attempt to release the starlings failed, that it took at
        least two or three attempts for the starlings to mate and
        multiply,

how he struck hard and harder to acclimatize the starlings so
   they would stick. Strange, as this bit of information would
   have made your own story more tragic,

made the man a bit more sinister for his vigorous approach to
   an entire evil. To rub it in a little more, you might have
   mentioned, too, the act,
line, and scene in the Shakespeare, quoting Hotspur in *Henry
   Four One*, vowing to make a starling wreak and repeat the
   name
Mortimer in the ear of the king, *to stir his anger*, to enrich his
   ire. How this would have made Schieffelin and his damage
   even more ridiculous,
his drawing a living army of Shakespeare's birds with little or
   no attention to their meaning or significance in his craze
to make a live concordance of birds taken from books. Sure,
   there was your general, dull warning about the extensive
   effects
of one man's motions upon our mass of environment. There
   was even your noise about the famous jaw. Yet you made
   no connection, in your firm and final cautionary, between
   Hotspur's sore
urge, that fantasy from which the starlings were taken, and
   what has become of us, how we are all kings with harried
   ears, really, waiting for the wailing to stop.

REST AFTER

I am on the road when she passes, as they say. The news arrives
by phone, so I skip her house, driving straight to the hotel and
　　into bed.
Wired from the driving, though, and spent, I do nothing but spy
the two retrievers there – one golden, and one an almost bottle
　　red –
my father's cousin's dogs roam that house, straying, even, in-
　　between
the legs of nana's stretcher. She rises a little, then, set out
and centred in her living room, delivering the last or just about
the last, full sentence she is reported to have said, which gets
　　taken as the keen
proof of her iron humour – that wry, fantastic wit she honed
over the course of the Great Depression. *Get out of here, and shut
　　the lights
on your way out*. No one takes her at her word, or, wanting to
　　show
their own unwillingness to have her have her way, they carry
　　out their last defiances
then and there. The favourite lamp still blinks, and most who
　　mind,
in any case, are gathered when the night nurse calls the time.

THE END OF THE NOVEL

Though it belongs to everyone dwelling here,
and all claim it as their own, this is not a country.
The lovers here are tortured by their orthodoxies
and appearances. They both cheat. One so we can see it,
heaving and raw during his brief exile in America,
the other, only in retrospect, as evidenced in her
accumulation of material objects and her more staunch
religious devotion. When they come together,
having found themselves wanting, after all,
their reunion is supposed to appear high ecstasy
against the background of an embattled Israel,
the amphitheatre of fiction itself. Whatever kernel
of romance the author would convey remains
spoiled, though, for all their initial, heavy cheating –
too much representative of the war after all,
though perhaps it was meant to be so. In another,

the problem is not love in excess but its
extinction in installments. There's the initial
passion, but someone else, angered by it,
in the old fashioned way, sends one of the lovers
away against their will. When they meet again,
the pair's diffident. They appear alienated from one
another. Though only a quick diffidence is allowed
before they are lost in a bombing – more dreadful
because its sound is muted in the excitement over
the end of the war. All this is supposed to sore trumpet
again when we are told the reunion itself is a sham.
It has never happened, the lovers coming together, at last,
not their dying together, either. This last bit, as it turns
out, is just the villain's therapeutic, part of the new
trauma revealed to us in the epilogue. I find

I am the woman in the third. Kidnapped by an ex-
boyfriend, a sex maniac who claims I am his first
and only love, I appear dull, obviously not much
of a catch because my memory's fagged out, and I'm
trotting around his back parlour an amnesiac, applying
makeup on the hour (I've turned ugly or perhaps I
always was). No matter my appearance he can't help
trying to convince me he's done something very real
for us, even or especially as I make my escape. That he
also claims my adopted son's his own's easily conceived.
He's had half a universe of women, after all, and he's
desperate. Though the point's that he's diminished neither
by my going nor the death of my son that's his loss now, too.
No, the point's that after all these attempts to betray us out
of our senses, he makes a healthy conversion, if only a slight
one, to frank, old mysticism, finding some statue endowed

with the same little spirit that pervades them all. Having
read them, now, and experienced this last in more
than the ordinary fashion, I am equipped to speak on behalf of you
novelists, tell you that your capitals, romance, and realism
have broken up at last and gone into hiding. Do not leave it
to poetry to reunify them, ask for the live space of the lyric
or the sonnet as your alternative, say, superior, transport here.
Sacrifice your own. Send your children out (like the kids
of the big movie stars, yours are bound to amplify themselves,
as well, in your fame and fortune) searching with the old
pitchfork and scythe. Get a few good hurricane lanterns and go
back hunting for a moral and a bind for the good organ's
writhing in this rush to make the psyche, callow personage,
promiscuous as an old miser in one of his jangling hypos.

A MUSCLE IN THE COUNTRY

This man who made a million as a minor
rock star in the eighties, one of those muscles
with fluorescent hair and an electric bass,
speaking, now, with a little renewed authority

(he's made a comeback as a minor
television star) pronounces in his muscled
voice to the local radio host, his deep-throated bass
ripped and uncut, that he's taken authority.

He's done it, he says, he's gone and bought a farm.
The city, it seems, doesn't offer enough value
for his passing dollar. And he's smart
about his money now. His million, no, not at all,

his million won't buy anything comfortable here. But a farm
in the country, you can be assured of its value.
A good fifty acres is worth (and he's smart –
anything less than fifty acres would be no country at all,

nothing to drive your snowmobile over
and get lost into) the expense.
It used to be that an estate
was extremely difficult to manage.

Men of little business sense, landed fools the world over
knowing little or nothing about the expense
of country living, had to give over their estates
for the sake of economy, would have to manage

themselves into a security by running away to the city,
enabled, there, to make some show

at little or no cost. They'd retrench,
sublet their great country houses so as to reappear

in the face of urbanity, there, in the city,
endowed and terrific. Today, though, the land is mostly show.
No need to be worked for profits. No need to retrench.
No men with bills who appear and reappear

upon your doorstep. No depending on your tenants
either, no rents on which to base your living.
Today, there are exports and greenhouses. Grow
anywhere, exchange it, and get what you want.

For instance, there are cows in Japan, tenants
of luxury, feeding on beer and oats, living
in bunkers the size of toothpicks but growing
fat in their daily massages. Those cows get what they want,

and so do we. We're smarter about things. For a piece
of land, he says, the size of a barn or with a little extra,
a parcel the size on which a mule might wander,
but in the place of the agricultural, you can expense,

if you are careful, a new house, a garden, and a piece
of wilderness. The country's cheap and with a little extra
effort, it might just get you happy. You might even wander
yourself into something spectacular if you expense

some extra time and a little of your own effort
returning your empire of sod to the forest that it was before
farming, that is, and the people destroyed it. When he's settled,
he says, that is what he will have, a place bee-stung

with recreation. He's alright. He just wants his efforts
kept somewhat quiet, in the end, though nothing before
you ever really goes dead-quiet in the country. All unsettled
there, he knows, nature buzzes and stings.

And, on his new front porch, cutting somewhat of a minor
figure, he might just allow himself, he says, the muscles
in his arms pumped as he turns out his new, acoustic bass,
to think the birds cried out to meet him there in his authority.

ANNOTATIONS ON YOUR PASTORAL, *SUMMER*

It's true. There is some heaven or delight in this hot landscape,
   though the gods of love and war have not descended. They
   never do. Those voices you hear behind the patch of trees
   are only investors bidding on a piece of land they're going
   to improve.
As for the men walking through the fields, *crowned with corn*,
   as you put it, there's nothing silent about them. All sweaty
   and broken, they're swearing their way from the
   glassworks. Though I grant you it might be better if they
   were singing some common song or silent as tombs.
Drawing from these, you say that you've come to realize that
   your love for me is a viper in your chest or, as you
   mentioned earlier, an incurable disease. We've all indulged
   our tastes enough to acknowledge that there's a certain
   sweetness or pathos in a wrecked man. Still, I've left you
   with some purpose. Let's say the fountains were mouldy
   and the grasses all burnt.
But here's too much. Imagining me back again, you say that I
   would be the cause of certain beneficial changes in the
   climate. With me, the summer would bear less heat,
   breezes would travel in my wake, flowers launch their
   pistils and stamens higher so that the old garden would
   flourish and form a shade. That's not what I'm about.
Sure, if I came to you, singing, the few wondering trees might
   shake their heads and lower the temperature a few
   degrees, but the mountains' and streams' cheap echoes
   wouldn't make the night fall any sooner for all their air
   and cool.

OF MINOR FIGURES

for Carleton Wilson

---

sum wudewe wunode oswyn gehaten	a certain widow called oswyn dwelt
æt þæs halgan byrgene on gebedum	near the burial place of the saint in prayer
and fæstenum manega gear syððan	and fasting for many years afterwards
seo wolde efsian ælce geare þone sanct	she would each year cut the saint's hair
and his næglas ceorfan syferlice mid lufe	and his nails soberly with love
and on scryne healdan to halig-dome on weofode	and keep them in a shrine for relics on the altar

In Ælfric's *Life of Saint Edmund*,
before the thieves come to prey upon the templed body,
to establish that the saint is indeed saintly,
the author meditates for a while, delivers

this canny description of the widow Oswyn.
In Ælfric's *Life of Saint Edmund*,
beside silver and gold jars
that establish the saint is indeed saintly,

she fasts and prays with conviction.
This canny description of the certain widow Oswyn:
trimming Saint Edmund's fingernails and hair, storing them
in silver and gold jars –

How much power she exercises, they'd say *anweald*,
fasting and praying with conviction.
As she manages the brilliant body of Saint Edmund,
trimming his fingernails and hair, storing them as relics,

aside from the saint himself, and his guardian wolf,
how much power she exercises, they'd say *anweald*,
gathering the relics, ensuring Edmund's beatification.
As she manages the brilliant body of the saint,

though her description makes for a relatively short passage in
     the *Life*, she is,
aside from the saint himself or the guardian wolf,
wouldn't you say, the most important figure in the story,
gathering the relics, ensuring Edmund his beatification.

In fact, does she not stalk the story, as she stalks us now?
Though hers is a relatively short passage in the *Life*, she is,
she does, usually, overpower us a little.
Wouldn't you say that the most important person in the story,

not because she appears, at first, as a marginal, (that's so passé –
in fact, doesn't she stalk the story, as she stalks us now?)
as a minor figure to be brought to the centre later,
usually does overpower us a little?

And that those widows and blind men who hallow the saints
not because they appear, at first, as marginals (that's so passé),
occasion the miracles, soberly, and with love?
She is not some minor figure to be brought to the centre later.

She stalks the story as she stalks us now, a first state
of the many widows and blind men who hallow the saints
in the lives of the saints. In their *anweald*, they
occasion their miracles, soberly, and with love.

A BRIEF TOUR OF THE AVENUE

It is irritating. The roots of these black walnuts
devastate whatever else you plant in the ground
around them. Forget putting anything below.
Their shade, too, you can just as easily forget.
Sitting there in the cool will only send you
into the house with a headache. That is no old
wives' tale. It's true. Just coming within a few yards
of a black walnut tree (and we have this avenue)
can make you sing out for your bottle of pills.
I suppose we like them, then, for the shadows
they cast on the house or for how they make us go
around and about them to reach the front door.
We usually pass by the borders, the day lilies
or the vegetables instead, and all that error makes
for good conversation. I suppose we like it, too,
for the musty walnuts we gather here, occasionally.
As for these, there is very little getting at them.
Outpace the crows and the tree rats, catch
what has been dropped below before your head
starts reeling, and you are still faced with
drying them in the sun, and husking them, too,
maybe by running over their green bodies with
your car in reverse or by beating them hard
and rolling over them with a pin and board.
After that, you sort out the few whose shells
don't appear worm-eaten and have your go.
There's usually, you will find, a couple worth
the effort. And that is how you will remember them,
by the effort. No matter how long the fragrance
lingers on your palate, from the work alone, from
the getting, your hands will stay green for weeks.

THE COURSE OF THE RENOVATIONS

I.   Transformation AGO
     The Art Gallery of Ontario

Though there are hardly any signs of transformation, though
the few architectural plans posted on the pillar appear blurry
and suspicious, it is no matter. You are still on for renewal.
The renovations they are staking here are bound to shift your
notion of spectacle. And you plan to come again, some time
after the official gala, around noon or on the free nights
if they still have them (what with the expenses) to judge
the standards and the borrowed pieces, too. After being moved
into the expanded galleries, those paintings you know or knew
might even be said to move you differently, placed in more
challenging configurations and offset by the Thomson gifts
and the temporary loans. With the daylight or the free nights
spooning through the enlarged windows and the promised glass
roof, this all might even make the most substantial contribution
to Canadian oils and statuary since the artists first produced
the works themselves. You wonder if you might not just marvel,
in and among your standards, then, your Group of Sevens
and your Québec fires, your Inuit hunters, fishing or owling
fish, sometimes followed by fleets of kids in canoes, marvel,
even after the shine wears off and you grow accustomed
to the changes, if you do. Waiting for your eyes to adjust
to a certain night piece, that one oversized work in oils
(you always had to wait for it, if only to misconstrue) you
might just finally come to know the nature of the accident
that happened there, along the river, by the tracks, see why
the few remaining people can be seen running away on the tar
water, away from the scene or from the noisome maritime bleak
pressed in upon them there and licking at them from the sides.
Or you might improve just in reconsidering the plain
character of Varley's kneeling girl, *Dharana*, once again.

ii.   Renaissance ROM
      The Royal Ontario Museum

It is all thinking in general. The rust on the foundation
materials, the orange acid acting or reacting on
the surface of the steel pillars, fixes me. And I stop
to wonder if that rust will seep through the steel and mar
the whole extension to the side of the museum, that crystal,
eating at it from the roots, or if it is just the general nature
of these parts (of which I know very little) to look used
and worn even before their first propping up. It is all
thinking in general. The men in hard hats, hanging from thick
cords, saddle the pillars and weld the impossible angles
of the new addition. They are magnetic. As always, people want
to walk below and beside them. The crew has even cut holes
for windows in the wooden safety walls, to sate us all
from a safer distance. I am sure if any one of these work-
men whistled down to me, I would speed my way to him
(and you would, too), though they all appear too stuck
in their work to notice. When I pass again, as I manage
often in my excitement over the course of the renovations,
I think on their forebears setting the greater bridges
of the twentieth century, the ones, according to the social
histories, who lost or faced losing their families every day,
and in far more hazardous conditions than these. Thinking
modernity, for all that it improves, never does away with risk,
I tremble for these newer men now, too, as if I might be one
of their own relations and I feel I might experience a particular
kind of suffering should one of them falter, or fall near me
or in my own line of vision. But this is all thinking in general.
This far, there have been no serious accidents, no grave cases.
And that steel will hold for ages per the architect's design,
despite the film of rust that can be seen along its sides.

THE WIFE OF PILATE

When he was set down on the judgment seat,
his wife sent unto him, saying, 'Have thou nothing
to do with that just man: for I have suffered many
things this day in a dream because of him.'
   – Matthew 27:19

From my husband, I learned a little something of duty,
and he caught something from me in return. A shock
of hair and feathers shuttled along the floor beside
our breakfast table yesterday as he spoke, still, low,
about his own, about the cleansing of hands, the newly
irrigated fields down the river, spread with dead or de-
programmed fish, and the new annex to the city,
a calendar of homes already sinking into the sand.

Perhaps out of duty, I wanted to see this place he knew
without having stepped a foot outside of the capital.
So I travelled the river, low at this time of year. My legs
spread apart, my skirts hitched around my waist and over
my shoulders so I could see my knees, I felt the grasses skin
my shins. I watched the fish succeeding me, arrowing ahead
and flashing behind like the coloured protons and neutrons
on the pages of our outdated textbooks, old drawings of the atom.

I waded long and never spied that city, only groups
of washerwomen or just their piles of rags
on the side of the water, drying in the sun,
suits of clothes torn up now for housecleaning
or to be made over for the poor. We'd never have this
at home. He never lets a thing run down so as
to divide it among his fellows, and I'm so experienced
now, I can't escape his *règles du jeu*, or my own.

You'll go and say it was a dream. I certainly wanted it
to be one. As I was taking my rest under a lime tree,
preparing myself to come back here, disappointed
with the city that never materialized or had already
sunk (all of this probably suggesting he had a fancy
or at least business somewhere I knew little about)
I looked up at those branches – they offered some uncertain shade –
and spotted a hawk looming. What I would have given

to have been a kind of Leda then, for that bird
to have flown down and made a supper of me
or come all over my leg, lifting a cold god
from my thigh. And with my longing the bird
raised its wings on edge. But it was a hawk in wings
only that clambered down on top of me, a hawk
with the face of a man, the paws and tail of a lion
(or one of those cloned sheep) connecting himself to me

in a nauseous instant. And it wasn't sex he'd come for
or anything like it, but a fight towards a death
of a sort I could barely master – his wings flashing,
his punishing my side with that tail that sent
cross charges circling around my stomach.
And despite his blue-eyed, swollen, pitiful look,
despite his eyes full of remorse, not for anything
he had done, though, perhaps for what I wanted, I hid

my fear and my own pity, and matched his stinging with my
fists and my unbolted knees until blood censored
from the holes where his feathers had stood –
glistening. In return he drew hold of me, blasting
my neck and my eye, using his tongue against me,
that short, barbed thing – another sort

of lash. It bristled me to the teeth. So we fought,
the ruddy afternoon, the night, one half day of nothing

I'd call paradise or even close, rolling, and pausing,
sometimes giving way for breath, but even then,
alert or at least allergic, combative. He'd be at his least
victorious when I'd levy away, when I showed signs
of giving over and sinking it all. 'Til, in an instant
(you might say, one of love), he loosened his grasp,
his tacking me down, and pled with me to bless him.
For all my bloody body I could not fathom

what it was he meant. Unless it had to do with
his eyes changing into screens, broadcasting
the skeleton of a new city, seven steel buildings,
standing and disappearing in an instant,
or the pictures in the thunder I made on his chest,
blueprints for what looked like a metropolis,
already dashed, sinking into his body or into the sand
around us. So I blessed him, as I do my husband

every morning at the sink in the rear of our house.
I drew water from the river, filling the crook
of his right shoulder, or where I imagined his shoulder
to be. Taking water from this makeshift hold,
I raised my middle and ring fingers to his forehead,
signing a figure eight – two scrolls. With this, he drew
his feathers from my hair, drew them across his face
and wept. I understand little of this whole scheme, except

I'm hardly bruised and I can hardly show for it. So,
when you go to my husband, down by the prison there,
notwithstanding his pride, tell him I've suffered

much over righteousness or some righteous person
today in a dream. And tell him that I'm standing
at the door of our house, or in the basement, anxiously
following the reports online, that I'm willing to welcome him
home in his urgency, when he returns, in spite of all this.

NOTES ON IMMIGRATION

Some voyages out, some immigrations have been fruitful,
curing or encouraging faith. When Scottish soldiers shook
their pillows and abandoned their ship mattresses, the heather
they used as ticking broke free and seeded itself over half
of Atlantic Canada, an unexpected comfort for the Scots
who settled there that comforts us today. Though many immigrants,
they say, behave differently here, especially in the less
temperate zones. They do not sink their taps into the soil,
as if for good. They only drop their seeds. A new plant
each year. You will see the son of the son, the annual,
but never, as the plants diversify, the father returning.

My husband writes about an art professor he knows
who spends his free hours shooting the non-native birds
that dare fly over his property. On the whole, this professor
remains a careful man. To minimize his taxes he has made
each room in his house appear, effectively, an artist's space.
I imagine, though, one day, this doctor might succumb
to one of those accidents so frequently rendered
by Frost as typical of the agricultural scene.

For the most part, the famous become known
as spenders of nature. The kudzu, that vine
from the east, made its way to the American south
as a leaf on the shoe of a passenger on a trading vessel.
That leaf set out and swiftly strangled a little life
out of the woods, secluding the more secluded houses
in sheets and shingles of acid green. The zebra mussels
who stuck themselves to those spice boats, too, are now
sticking to our local water mains. This season, the Asian
longhorned beetle has cheated half of Toronto of its shade
trees, though those trees, themselves, were imports once.
Once, they robbed a slew of goldenrods of the sunlight

they needed to thrive. And now the yellow wisps,
the goldenrods that hold the eggs the crickets eat or set
upon them there so as to thrive are also less in number.

Now we will have to spend a stretch of time grieving
for the talking birds, the crested mynahs, brought
to Vancouver, once, by a bunch of entertaining salesmen.
Freed from the people who imported them there
where they never would have had the energy to fly,
the mynahs, those fantastic mimics, at once appeared
a relaxed species. They were one of the few kinds of birds
who did not seem to mind leaving their eggs unprotected
as they spanned out to forage for food. Today, as far
as the birders can tell, those fantastic creatures who once
startled you by calling out to you in your own voice
were out-competed by that menace, the starling.
I can understand why you might want to shoot those
manic competitors who took the mynah's nests
as the mynahs themselves wandered lackadaisically,
I can see how you might want to take a couple
of starlings out in order to extend to them your grief.

The same might be said of certain people though,
so the urge needs minding. Whenever splendid rewards
are to be had, accolades, say, in the arts and sciences,
and certainly, in the reverse, in those times when threats
crop the general population, the general population tends
to look among the immigrants, in search of the next
potential star or perpetrator. They say you can usually find
the artist and the immigrant in the same or similar quarters
of the town. Those of us who claim to be both will have
to take particular care. They say, in our most beautiful
advances as in our terrible prognostications, it is the lot

of the artist as the immigrant, in body or in mind, never
to fully adapt, not even out of love, but to be killed or,
as he or she finds it in their power, to kill and to consume.

A NEWER WILDERNESS

We are astonished with our capacity to alter
the world's evolving, not only the damage
or salvation we wreak upon the environment,
but through this apparent meddling, the slight
yet substantial ways we modify language, law,
and human sympathy. A bottle dropped in the wilderness,
or into the sea, or an uncharacteristic clamour in a voice
that is just calling for another cold drink in all this humidity
thrill us with their potential for shifting
the nature of things, keep us contemplating
our inevitable decay, or worse, the decline of culture –
as in that Bradbury story, in which a man,
returning from a dinosaur hunt, exits the time-
travel office to find his world altered,
because at one point on his hunt, he stepped
off of the path and a butterfly stuck to his shoe,
almost dead, writhing. Reading this,
we are thrilled to parse out our ascendancy
over this fool of a man who paid to see and shoot
a dying animal. Then there is that shock
in our discovering that his slightest movement
from the pathway really did astonish the elements,
though not the landscape or the course of the weather,
but certain habits, or habits that once seemed certain
though they never really could have been: that man's
own reading, writing, spelling, his speaking with a tickle
in his throat, his kind of attitude. It is true enough,
but not entirely true, that we transform this earth,
some by pummelling, and some as willing to save seed,
and that our physical and intellectual habits are hardly
immune to this taking from or drawing into
the finest greenery. Still, our hold on decay is hardly
in dominion. As if the sunlight flashing on the egg

of an unconscious spider won't, alone, awake
a new poison in all its perfusion, as if Nature
or Nature's God, with all of these fribbling atoms,
does not recreate a newer wilderness in us
and in our languages before we have roused
ourselves to damn and hail our sway.

II

KENOTAPHION

Time's the king of men,
He's both their parent, and he is their grave,
And gives them what he will, not what they crave.
    – Shakespeare, *Pericles, Prince of Tyre*, II.iii

I.   ARRIVED AT EPHESUS

Pericles III.ii

That this tar-heavy coffin and this woman's body,
dead from its own labour, could be so heavy
and yet still float. That the ocean would forfeit
this guerdon – those gems still startling through
her closed lids, the epitaph, a scroll
fitted into her clenched fist, that fist
poised to endure – rather than drowning her
and winning her over for a constancy,
for good. *Bury this woman, dead in child-*
birth. We couldn't keep her body and the boat
in the storm. Also consider her husband's
loss, or the grief of her father, and be kind.

If the ocean had only considered the misery
of a Pericles, taking a wife in its vast body,
in kind, she might have remained unconscious,
dead for once and for certain. Or at least,
in that airtight box, in and upon the water,
she might have woken to remember the birth
some hours previous, the infant body she yielded
only to the air and to its own patience. And surely,
if not with fondness then with very little spite,
she should have died again, forever, and for good.
But see how the ocean's thrown her up, become
an empty grave for all its spreading. Nothing

left now but to wake her, brush the fillet of gold
already breaking from her unstrangled lashes.
What a relief, if she immediately stood
and delivered herself to the temple here.
What a relief, if she were to up and propose
herself certain and celibate for the local deity –
for how can we suggest to this woman, belched up
from an unwilling ocean, suddenly awake,
that if she chooses to rest again, to return
to sleep as a means of recovery or to express
an immediate sense of mourning, she might very well die,
for sure and forever, right here, and in front of us?

II. HERALD

Matthew 28:1-7

Here's some angel, pectoral muscles
the size of human heads, lumbering up
the side of the hill, making heavy of it.
Here's a body Blake would have died for,
would have etched over and again to underscore
our own very diminutive nature
and all our wants, blue veins writhing.

Here he is apologizing as he bows,
making himself known to the gardeners
and the guards who scatter or are levelled
by the land, shaking. Here he is, struggling
to bend low enough to loosen the stone
that covers the tomb, then sitting on
that stone, cross-legged, mindful of himself.

You would think that with this kind
of a body, it would be easier to battle
some grotesque allegory of sin, any one
of our moderns, monstrous, conspiratorial,
than to lie in wait for two grieving
women, widows of a sort. Some mechanic
battle seems easy compared to this stopping

for two Marys come looking only for what's haggard
and broken here. For two Marys who have imagined
only the comfort and salve they might bring
to one failed body, on this of all mornings,
to be greeted by a mammoth! Save some

sympathy, then, for the mammoth who sits
making the tomb look smaller, this bulk

by his looks alone, come to tell these women
there's no body in the tomb, suggest to them
even, that it's risen, awake. For a moment, then,
pity the brute who must shock the women,
making them acknowledge their capacity
for felicity in the presence of a grief not
easily fathomed, though it continues to return.

III. AUBADE

Tobit 7-9

Before you woke, I went to pray at the window
almost as usual: *Take me out of this earth,*
I still hear their reproaches. Except the smell
of burnt fish roused me out of it. I stopped
to watch my father in the field beside the house
with his buddies from the town, filling in
the grave they dug in the night. He was drunk.
He kept climbing in and out of the hole
waving a piece of parchment paper, our
marriage license. Once, he lay flat in the grave.
Then he rose into a sitting position, hallooing.
The men roared and then took turns pushing
him in and pulling him out again.

They had loosed the goats, too. They milled
around, disoriented, near the graves
of the seven husbands I already buried.
Once they'd mated, multiplied, but at some
point, they'd all become of one age, too old
to bear or to be eaten. The goats that morning
seemed particularly hungry, starved, nipping
at the heels of the men who stood on
the furthest edges of my father's posse.
The goats looked as if they, too, had been up
half of the night, minding the diggers
as they handled their shovels, waiting
for one of the women to shriek.

Far away from the others, near a woodpile,
your cousin Azarias, that hulk who looked

nothing like the rest of your family (has he ever
resurfaced?) bent over to gather four fingers full
of mud. He smeared his cheeks with the stuff.
No one called to him. He was not recognized,
nor did he want to be seen. Though later, during
the wedding breakfast, he'd claim that overnight
he destroyed something sinister, some demon
foreigner – so you would not die like the others,
so this marriage might take. I still don't believe him.
None of those other deaths resulted from some spirit's
conniving, nor is your living that kind of miracle.

Downstairs, something broke, a plate, maybe,
or a bottle of wine. I could hear the women circling,
irritating each other with all of their attempts
to keep silent, fumbling with their kitchen tools.
How they must have counted on it being spoiled.
Hadn't they grown used to these breakfasts as wakes?
But parts slid together. My father shrieked his last
halloo, climbing out of the hole with his shovel.
The goats ran like kids into the hills, bleating.
I heard Azarias lumber into the kitchen, encouraging
the women to clean him up, giving them some purpose.
And your little dog leapt to my ankles, cowering,
as if he, too, knew what was going to happen,
that we would be spied, against the window, by a deep-
breathing man collecting his first full wash of sun.

IV. SWEET SPICES

Mark 16:1-4

Why couldn't this have been more slapstick?
Three hefty women carrying their equal weight
in groceries and linens shoved up against
their breasts or slung over their shoulders,
three horse-strong women barking at each other
about how heavy the door over there is, and who's
going to bother to open it once they get to the house.

You'd see Mary, sunburnt, carting a tub of aloe
on her left shoulder, fixing a braid with her free
hand, saying, *no, not me*, as she shoo-shoos
a pigeon from the sidewalk in front of her, then James'
mother, the little Mary, almost upending herself
as she bends over to swat at the first Mary's pant-
leg, saying, *I'm not touching that door*. She's trying
to remove a leaf that's caught on the ankle, swatting
at it with her box, a box half the size of her own body.
The leaf's still sticking as big Mary walks, and the spices
in the little one's box, cinnamon and cassia, keep slipping
out at the sides, followed, sometimes, by larger,
gummed-up pellets of myrrh. For a moment, it looks
like little Mary's shaking her spices out purposefully
over the sidewalk, as you'd mill icing sugar over
the top of a cake for decoration. Salome, swaggering,
brings up the rear, thinking the spices smell sweeter
in the outdoors. She remembers a story about a queen
who had herself embalmed in cinnamon when she died.
How she made the whole town cover their bodies and blanket
their walks in layers of spice. How they kept it up for years

after her passing, a sign of honour. They say the demand
for cinnamon opened up trade routes there. So Salome's *fagged
out*, too busy rooting her nose in her basket of linens,
thinking tonight's the night she might finally play sweet
in bed, play dead to make him think she's winsome.

Wouldn't it be better if the butt of this whole thing
was that those women were able, even with all
of their packages, to open that door, but that they
were just too lazy? With all this, wouldn't it be
sweeter, then, for them to find the door already
open when they got there, to watch them drop
their heavy parcels, maybe knocking each other over,
before they entered the house, rearmed with pots
and rolling pins, ready to attack the robbers?

V. PRAYER TO A HEROINE OF ROMANCE FOR A BETTER MEMORY

Pericles IV.i

Having been nursed on stories of your birth seems
to have increased your capacity to remember,
keeps the knives recoiling from your white
throat, the throat of a paragon, a throat that continues
to release songbirds in its turn. Some other
heroines go as far as to remember the formation
of the stars or the kind and colour of the flowers
that bloomed the morning of their birth. With these
odd snatches of history, told to them by their nannies
or nurses, the accomplished save themselves
from spinsterhood, retrieving the men they've lost
to clowns, female ambassadors, or demanding
fathers. But you're tops with this phenomenon.
Why ask anyone else?

       Nothing escaped your nurse, and you can tell
the wind was north when your mother died.
The night of your birth, your father cried, *good
seamen*, clung tight to the mast like a toddler
to a mother's skirts, clung to the mast with a king's
hands because that tempest had already been fed
your mother's body. You tell and even repeat
to yourself how your father stood on a deck half-
bursting with ocean. And it does not escape you to herald
what the canvas climbers said or how they whistled
down to match the water's confusion.

                              If you hadn't
been taken off the morning Leonine moved
to trace an artery in your neck, your memory

would have saved you anyway. When he asked you
to pray your last, you did not say you could not
remember doing any harm but that you could recall –
clearly, you'd never spoken a harsh word, never crushed
a mouse. And this was true, this carefully netted
register of your faultlessness – sweet enough
to save you. Or if it was not, quite, your reminding
Leonine he had a gentle heart would have kept him
from harming you, even if the pirates had not seen
you standing there, rapt, and taken you off.

    Good Marina, despite the fact that I have
parents living, and close by, despite the fact
that despite their living, I still do not know the story
of my birth, not even the hour I was born – in my
recounting all of this, in my coming to terms here
with what is yours, grant me half as good a memory,
so I might escape this dying, too, a while longer.

VI. OLD ROAD

Luke 24:1-12

It was lumber, their treading,
no one looking up or over
at the sides, or if they looked,
all glazed and passive stares.
The women paced slow enough
but were far too interested
in their own conversation
to witness much, dropping
half of their supplies along
the way. They never saw
how their aloe and myrrh,
fallen, served to plug up
the wider crevices struck
into the path. Nor could they
mark it, running back
with unbelieving looks,
their eyes knocked open
but only giving out, not taking
in the scene. Not soon enough,
a single man sped by, almost
at a guilty pace, making for
the place where the women
were frightened. Was it that
he did not believe the story
they came to tell with their
shocked faces, or did he want
to see that kind of absence
for himself? In any case,
consider it only another
instance of the old denial.

It is an old complaint,
but I will make it anyway.
Had they looked up, or down,
or to the sides at any moment,
they would have known some-
thing or someone had come up.
Had they noted the ground here
was thick in places, broken
in others, that the palms bent
so low you might consider
climbing into one and being
catapulted across the city,
had they noted the wind
blew against the normal,
or that the sun, shaving off
the ridge like that suggested
more of an evening than day-
break, they would have saved
themselves too much amazement
and merely been amazed, they
would have saved themselves
some heavy time and a little
more perdition.

VII. EYE OF TOBIT

Tobit 11:7-15

In his basement, this genius of a kid
has rigged up a Museum of the Apocrypha
for Halloween. There's Holofernes' Head
hanging on the wall, looking as if it's
only just been cut off. And there's the Eye
of Tobit, moulded in plastic and set
in a coffin built to suit. Masterful,
the things kids create, though they don't know it.
That's what we say, but they're always aware.
Proud, the kid squirts paste on the eye he's made
(a freckle rimming the iris, just like
his dad's) to fake glaucoma. Then, magic.
He waves his rubber fish above the eye
and wipes off the gall so it can be seen again.

VII. IN THE GARDEN

John 20:14-17

You would not believe it was his daughter
either, if you sat with her as he sat through
the mandatories and the electives, if you
had watched her come out of *the convent*,
(their play on *l'hôpital or l'hôtel dieu*)
wrapped in linens, almost gone. You
would say it was some other child,
snatched, or kidnapped maybe for her looks,
brought in to replace the daughter or to atone,
milling in and out of the rose bushes there,
commenting that the roses he'd planted
at his daughter's birth smelled like cinnamon
and the ocean. That small girl's talking
to him about the roses and *his daughter's
birth* as if she were someone else's, and
older, all her grave words about the garden
and its growth chosen ahead of time, you
might think, to draw him out of his grief,
*like Patience on kings' graves, as we
have read, smiling extremity
out of act.* Your eyes would seem
suddenly moist and half-swollen, too,
if she came towards you, looking more
alive than your daughter ever did,
with her thumb pricked by some thorn
or tine she'd touched too gently
in the garden. With her bleeding hand,
her whole body smelling of cinnamon,
or the ocean, you would not believe

it was your daughter telling you not
to weep in front of her, and not to
touch her either, she could
not have your help this time.

IX. IMPERATIVE

Pericles V.i

My house is where my family and those
who admire me all meet together.
Go there, and talk about how you lost
the ones you loved, how you mourned
your losses with those of your friends
and came to find all that you had lost
awake and still breathing beside you.
Repeat all of this to them. Give it life.

Do not bother to talk about governments
or ministers, petty forms of religion
and state. Reveal everything else.
Speak about all that you craved
and all that came in its place.
Tell them that these long days
you did not stop to eat or drink,
but that you saw a vision.

III

DURING THE SPRING DANDELION RUSH IN IRVINE, CALIFORNIA

after William Cowper

Men made this town. There is barely any country in it.
I'm sure that here, on the side of the road,
in the weed patch between the marine base
and the mini-mart, here, where they can't build
because the helicopters must land safely,
you'd say there wasn't any virtue or health
in these drifts of hedges that uproot themselves
come fall and shuffle around town as tumbleweeds.

Though some sweet bitter draught might be
what they are after, those women in the short pants,
crouched down in the brush, picking dandelions,
their black trash bags spread out beside them, catching
wind, as if they were giant snails, slagging along the fens.
The women, pink and orange edges, holding down
their hideous, inflated shells (their bags doubling as weather-
cocks, then), in their stooping, stoop low, pulling
the yellow wonders from what is merely a wonderless,
fruitless open, taking them for salads and wine.

In the evening you can see them best. Some of them
even wear reflective jackets or set lanterns at their sides.
Then the moon spins softly, sets the weeds into relief,
and the women bend, stiffened, their bags silvering,
flexed. It's then that the clocks of the dandelions, the white
cottons that have matured or been re-sexed (useless
for vintage but the heart of next year's crop) get sifted out.
The women, picking the meatier, yellow greens for wine,
blow the silks away. The clocks float by and shift
across the landscape as if the women had let loose stars
from the earth and flushed them out to bless the motorists.

The clocks, the unwanted, seedy white termagants,
bound to plant themselves again and grow more weeds
jet across the windshields of the night drivers who dart
by in their sedans, thinking they know no fatigue but idleness,
appearing to taste nothing other than what sad, dull art
provides. How this thinking subsides during the short season,
when the men and women see the clocks' night-flashing,
the white weed curricles floating past, perhaps caught
in a wiper for a moment, scuttling along the dashboard,
snowing in the rearview mirror as they prepare to signal
and turn.

        After these initial encounters, some
of the drivers actually unleash themselves, though
only usually miles later, as they sense what they have
been wanting, that arch of empire the women steal over them
in their plucking and blowing away. And they begin to ask:
how do those women travel there? And how do they stand
to bend there, crouched all day? How is it their labours pay,
or do not, for the life of the city? What cure comes
from the drink and would it be worth the expense?

And in this after-mirth or retraction, swelled
from the place we call country, the women's act
of plucking and sifting brings public mischief, as along
the roads, the accidents happen a bit more frequently
than usual. In neighbouring towns, miles past the base,
or along the main highway, the drivers struggle to relieve
themselves from their sense of warmth and humiliation.

Life, or some hiccough in its semblance, bursts inside
of them. It happens and they brake, or their feet
give out and they feel a rushing towards a living in the land,

imagining themselves in orchards, picking oranges, gun-
watering rows of cabbages, stretching plastic wrap
over lengths of strawberries to create a greenhouse effect,
then clutching at those dandelions, releasing their white
clocks to shiver in the night air.

                        There's that release,
until they fix their vehicles or buy new ones to prove
they have survived these crashes. There's that release,
until the winds move on and the summer drags in,
burning what's left of the weeds.

A CHILD'S GARDEN

One day, in and amidst the expanse
of this garden, mine, you will ask,
markedly, assured, *to plant and tend
and reap* your own plot.

And there will be no question.
You will have it. It is possible you
will choose some neglected spot
in our own yard, a hill in need

of fixing. You will dig it over,
ridding the soil of earthworms,
making the dirt more difficult,
so the native plants, the sumach,

the goldenrods, and the agrimony
might prosper, flourishing again,
as they would have, once,
in their wild nativity. Or, instead,

you might make over one
of those idles by the train
tracks, near where old Enelio
puts his renegade crops,

things too human, he says,
for a proper city garden. There,
you will stake your own victory.
No doubt, at first you will plant

too much, a smattering of everything.
But soon you will have your
favourites. You might take up,
for instance, one of the proven methods,

using a needle to inject cold
water into the folds of your
pumpkin vines, producing
a number of living giants.

From one of these boats, all
hollowed out, or from a teepee
thick-strung with provider beans,
you will run out, yourself

unstrung, to pummel
the commuter trains with crab-
apples plucked from the crab-
apple tree sprung up quick

in the corner there. A tree,
they will ask. A tree fruiting
young and profuse? Again,
you will have taken on too much

in the beginning – most gardeners do.
But with you, your excesses
are bound to pay off. In any case
it will put muscle on your shoulder,

this casting out your garden.
It will stand as one of your life's
great mysteries, too, one
you will speak about for years

to come, each time, sure stopping
to tell how amidst this sure
profusion, you always stopped,
you knew, to beg the seed.

LAZARUS SPEAKS IN FRONT OF LEMIEUX'S
LAZARE, 1941

The first sounds were nothing new. I had grown
accustomed to my wife and those other women issuing
graveyard prayers that rang even louder than the sharp wails
they initially sacrificed and flourished whenever a letter

arrived in place of a young man or his body, as if to console.
Even then, I was no young man. Though, as you might
expect, I would have given in to the impulse to shoot
anyone trooping in on our small province in search

of an easy stab at authority, the town treasury, maybe,
or one of its finer women. That day, they could have used me, too.
The beach was full of paratroopers plunging from the smoke
their aircraft embezzled over our shore,

troopers suspended and sailing from parachutes
made from their mothers' silk petticoats,
petticoats worn to social functions and then torn off,
just after marriage, in their fathers' matrimonial

heats, petticoats spun by silkworms in another
country their fathers' fathers conquered
long ago, with trade goods as arms.
From the top of that hill, I had a clear view

of the criminals shooting at our children. (For some
good reason, though I have forgotten that, too,
we bore them right up to the edges of the theatre.) Some
of my old schoolmates, in their Sunday hats

and zoot suits, gunned back at those intruders
with their hunting rifles. By the time I caught on,
the shooting was old. It looked as if my buddies,
firing like that, bored in their dress clothes,

meant to signal their stance against prohibition,
protection of the family swill and the right to still it,
rather than extermination in the entire. I, too,
was no saint, and it was better that they knew it.

As I rose up, I told the few mourners around me that I knew
I had died, or so it appeared, from a disease I contracted
from a foreigner during the first war. I finally succumbed,
or so I thought, to that numb death that choked up

my virility and all I was worth while my wife sat longing
for children, begging her God Almighty and the Virgin
to cure her ailment and fill her with life. I thought
it would be better if they knew all of that. Rising from my

coffin, I didn't want them to find my coming back to life
miraculous on account of any good I had been deserving
or had done, though I did not predict much awe
about the mourners, even then. Even as I held

my head up and reached for him, the second-best father
continued with his speeches. My wife and her sister
stuck to their prayers, despite what I had just revealed
about her barrenness being mine, and the grave

digger was calling already for silence from me
and from the covered wagon – that procession
of men in black approaching the old church plot,
recently enlarged, from below. Apparently, the digger

wanted the father to finish the service uninterrupted.
In my leisure, then, I looked down and saw, processing,
a half-dozen of my nephews and the local undertaker, fat
astride the hearse. What strange kind of mourning,

I thought, was that? Why would a funeral procession
follow upon a burial? Did they know they were coming
to take me up rather than batten me down? Had they
brought me once but then circled the town anticipating

I might be up again and in need of an ambulance?
And the most curious: after the prayers and the burial
service died down, how was it I could hear the pastor
speaking in the church on the hill, offering

a narrative of my short life and my failed honesty,
a reference to the disease I'd been hiding in his version,
too? He assured them all how little hope there was
for mine or any other's salvation. But still, he said,

the congregation might learn from my example, turn
to a kind of fruitful dwelling in this garden, despite
the chaos further east of us and our own sky raining
young men who were not our own, returning,

though some of us had our doubts. I knew then,
that the local church was still standing, blown open
but brimming with mourners half-listening to my life
drawn out in spades as little reason for personal

betterment, though as reason, still, for reform. The awe
then, was all mine. It was 1941. Even as I rose up out
of my coffin, it was not likely my funeral would stop
for me or for any other man surprised, then, to be living.

A NEWER WILDERNESS

There is something of the *deadlies* in that parallel
you made the other day, between total environmental decay
and the decline of language. It is out of character, really,
for you to make such an inadequate connection between
how we have abused world resources, how in all its wrath
of malformation and in its nuclear attitude, the earth
will beat back and thrash us with the poison we have been
feeding it for years, and how language, too, will burn out,
toxic, like our environment, dying in and among us, so
that even those words we use to name ourselves, or the most
basic human wants, will sound only as disconnected syllables
that mimic just three words after all: *trash or arm* or that
malady known as the *hypos*. As if decline would answer decline.
Least of all, you might have supposed that if the world
does come to burn, language will just become inflexible.
Its numbers or its breadth will not diminish. Our expression
will just stop changing, altogether, so that we will all
get stuck with the same accent, slinging the same slang
we have been slinging for years, the same sure words,
spoken in a singular manner, to attend to the world's
passing, to illustrate how we are just going to die
when we eat the grasses we learned to grow, finally,
from seed, in our sprayed-over, half-glowing gardens.
But this is not it at all. Don't you know that in and amidst
our own decline, our language will continue to build upon
itself, upon its own beauty – that suffering here, and spying
others dead, our expression will bound up and out like so
many wild, determined orchids, massing on our remains –
and amidst this profusion we will likely find more words
than we ever possibly imagined to describe what we have lost,
what, exactly, we require, and everything we cannot have?

THE MASTERS OF THE COUNTRY HOUSE POEMS

They are irreproachable, these poetical estates.
No amount of criticism could make them lose
their luster – fane and commonwealth, there's never
too much nostalgia about them or for their authors either.
In most, you will observe, the air is delicate
as it travels through the rooms' open keyholes,
swaying the unbolted doors ever so slightly. The whistling
corridors and the panelling, these are warmed only, yet,
as it stands, they are warmed entirely by the houses'
inhabitants in and after their prayers. The masters
in their verses never fail to invite the races to sit along
the lingering family tables filled and booming, here,
with flowers brought up from the local bottom.
Scads upon scads dip their bread in vinegar and oil
before taking a sip of the national beer. In these swell
places, fat is never begrudged, bullock thighs and steaks
the size of the yawning ruptures in some old miser's
older pants are passed around. The food even appears
to multiply in front of the poor, who, in these moments,
hardly appear poor at all – though they are poor – each
kitchen providing its temporary cure of goat's milk and kindness.
The churches close by could never give more than the masters
of these houses – the poets, I mean, not the masters proper,
but the poets who write of the giving here on these great estates,
these Penshursts and Saxhams owned by the best men
of the age, in which they once themselves were entertained.
These poets, they have understood, and their houses last.

They give and do not give. These houses, even without
their inhabitants, warm and providing, fend off heavy weather
more efficiently than anything on the market now, seeing
as they are, as has been said, the lilies of the umbrellas, the cases

of the turtle giants. And despite the fact that they will keep
open in all seasons, or because of it, our floods are nothing
to them. Yes. As the waters rush upon us, all biblical,
these are the kind of places that stand as beacons
in our minds, collecting us all from our makeshift rafts,
gathering us together, and bringing us to our senses again,
being, as they are and will be, the arks of a newer earth,
or if Jupiter had not already eaten here and decided to stay,
of another universe altogether. If you think about them hard
enough in your own suffering, you might even come to see
yourself standing inside of one of them, saved, your hand
stretched out of one of the open windows, waving its post-
diluvian triumph. If you think on them hard enough, these
great houses in their verses, you might even come to catch
your supper leaping at you from the waves below, a few bold fish
launched into your palm, in the great open manner of giving.

CERTAIN DISAPPEARANCES

There are few nuns these days, fewer cloisters.
Most women only travel among them to retire
to a still, remote location, after their husbands
pass away – or do not, for fear of insulting
their children, abandoning their neighbours.
The old material for romance has lost all
tenancy among us: no more eyeing girls
on the brink of settling into a life which cannot
return them to us individual – that moment
of crossing that is not movement but a word.

And Mary, all three Marys, stunning,
along the pews or in the formal galleries.
Their wrappings, the headdresses, the tunics,
no longer the brilliant precursors of this black
and white habit, long since relinquished.
The icons' robes, mere clothes again, or else
the garments you might see on women
in the coverage of one of our massacres,
pieces of cloth that hold their colour, soak up
blood, swaddle the dead if they're living a while,
or, as in the case of the Dormition, keep
them vivid while they are being entombed.

We are all too ready for the expected shock,
the report: *I am sorry to say they are gone now.*
The last nun's passed away with not one
sister and barely a priest to usher her on.
And if it bears no direct relation to a crime
or serious accident, those who do the reporting
will have to explain away this sudden-seeming loss.
Perhaps they will claim that those who might
have taken orders, once, became Unitarian

ministers, instead. Or, thinking historically,
that with the onslaught of what we still call
feminism, they married themselves to their wills,
became husband-men of the universities, went
corporate. And, to ease the burden awhile,
the reports will conclude, though consciously
mistaken, consciously though, that in any case,
most of us abandoned the church years ago –
to ease the burden for awhile.

                                    Not one
will attempt to explain this fundamental difference
in the atmosphere, though: the influx,
the corroboration of figures, hurtling close.
As occasionally as foul weather, we will
submit to the inevitable, half-naked bodies
of these once cloistered women, wrenching
the cities and prairies by night, tearing
at little girls by the bangs, tackling large men
and bending their elbows backwards. Stiff,
they will press their breasts into our backs, urging
not only glances but entire systems of gestures –
now bow, smack, or lift – upwards in us, and toward
the satellites. 'Til markedly, in time, they set
us loose, so we might glimpse their hale bodies,
barely scathed, punching forward in the draft.

CABBAGETOWN

There it is the green and green-yellow,
the cabbage flag. It looks like the back
of a little girl's head half-sprung with curls,
though dyed from its original blonde to the first
colour of nature. The green and green-yellow,
there it is, the cabbage flag, flying from most
of the houses here in this part of the city
known as Cabbagetown. Legend has it
the place got its name from the immigrants
and working people who came for the glass-
works and for work in other local industries.
They made do with the little land they set aside
for digging, planting vegetables in their front
and very public yards. In these their cabbages
were stars. Or even if they kept their planting
hidden at the back, on the first nights of fall,
which always surprise us with their chills,
chills colder than the chills of winter in all
their sudden, fall-like seizing, the streets here
would be filled with the warm-returning airs
of cooking cabbages, cabbages in stews
and broths or cabbages meant to be served
as sides to the occasional side of meat. You
could not say, here, that labour was not well fed.

You might say, though, the place has changed.
The people living here still work, I suppose,
but the smell of dinner, though it might wave on
luxurious, for all one knows, keeps or is kept
well within these homes, which are all about
the keeping. I love them, these houses,
their painted gingerbread, their scrubbed
bricks, and their reproduction fences – all fitted

to look more historically accurate than they
ever could have been. There is a fine
consistency about it all, even if it is a little
overdone. Well-loved, and well-preserved,
the birds, for instance, in the stained glass
windows set above the gas-lit entryways, they
blink the same cuckoos they have been blinking
for years. And in their care for these places they keep
ever so well and in keeping with the seasons,
the residents, as well, plant ornamental kales
and cabbages in the yards and laneways here.

You will find them in more hidden places, too.
Maybe you can just pick out that woolly head
peeking through the legs of the rose bush there,
or that kale brooding in the old milk door at the side-
entrance to number twenty-two, a door no one
there uses anymore but that they tend to decorate.
You would have to say these ornamentals hold
their own as they stand here through fall and pass
on into winter long and lanky on their stems, seeing
as they have not been cut. Even after their roots freeze,
they retain their colours, see, as if they were still living.
How could you miss this green-yellow body, half-
frizzled like a landed meteor, providing contrast
for the dogwood stems in the urn? The rouge
veins in this cabbage here, they throb just to look
at you and then go on to answer those, your own
long looks, in kind, with rushes of admiration.

> POET (*Preserve Our Eucalyptus Trees*) is a group that
> opposes the removal of eucalyptus trees. When their
> opposition refers to the eucalyptus as a 'giant weed'
> or an 'immigrant,' they call this attitude 'plant racism'
> or 'specism' and want it stopped before it spreads and
> gets entrenched in the minds of Californians.
> — Robert L. Santos, *The Eucalyptus of California*

It was a minor form of tyranny, supposed
to make us think twice about the place
of agriculture in the city. After they pulled up
the orange groves, leaving the trees' bodies,
limbs, roots, and all, piled on top of one another
on the edges of the roads, it was supposed to attack
our senses, their planting cabbage rows, the city
company. It was their way of instilling in us, driving
by that new expanse of quick commercial crops,
that vision of wealth and abundance, the idea
that it might just be better, then, to fill the space,
fill it to the brim with housing. Most times the air
was wretched, and this was what they counted on.
They wanted us turning up our noses at the unforgiving
cabbage stench, ourselves unforgiving. Jogging by
or driving in our cars on those cool and pleasant days
of early summer, confronted with what seemed at first
a mass of bitters in the air — this was meant to make us jog
the other way and roll our windows shut. With this they
thought we might just come to think it might be better
for the land and for us all if there were only houses there.

But most of us were peasants once and most of us are still.
And those cabbages, those ripe bustles in all of their
abundance made for too much fondness telling within,

what with our own live hunger and with our hunger increased
in remembering our fathers green with digging, the dirt
on their kitchen knives glistening green as cabbages, too,
as they stood in their back gardens, flushed from the pulling,
what with our fondness for the full cabbage dinners
that followed and at times still do. We had those dinners,
and we had our own intimacy with the land of California,
the earth and its breaking between our hands as we bent over
to make the smallest clearing, even if that clearing was meant
for nothing vegetable, nothing neat – only an annual bed,
say, or a cactus that never flowered, or an obedient plant
that hardly would obey. And when tested, our intimacy,
we would have to admit, extended far beyond those plots.

Besides, there were bodies, sweeter still, informing all
of this and set above us in our kind of bright content.
The eucalyptus trees the first men of the company
planted years ago in rows between the orange groves
as a keep-safe, a kind of windbreak or insulation
for the fruit, those other trees (some of us still
call them aliens) which served, in our time, to divide
the oranges from the fields of tract homes where most
of us grew up, those remaining trees, those hulking giants,
swaying fruitless and fat with carbon dioxide, fruitless
though they may have been, and ecologically termagant,
as we have been informed, they filled the air with their own
searching sweetness, as most of them still do, a living breath
which drew, as it draws now, the sugar from the other living things
nearby, all of our cabbages' air and cool. That boundary
of eucalyptus planted by the company, as long as it keeps
living (though it is likely, now, it will not be forgotten long),
keeps the others lingering, too, above our kind of bright
content (the whole of nature longs as well to hold) the last

bells of citrus from the upturned orange groves, and the mint- and orange-green belows of the company cabbages.

OPERA WEEK IN RADIO

Though the design is not medieval, the city's new opera house
    will look finest in the rain. It is vast, the box of glass and
    gray brick
built to protect the central core, that more solitary domestic,
    the theatre – itself designed to hold only five hundred or
    so as the music and the meaning are expressed
according to tradition or in some terribly modern way. No
    matter your seat, they say, you are bound to be touched
because of the sightlines and the acoustics. The music there is
    meant to meet the people outside too. We experienced this
    phenomenon ourselves
the week the CBC radio, hosted by Howard Dick, transmitted,
    live and at length, the company's interpretation of *Der
    Ring des Nibelungen*.

On Tuesday, labour's jangling Mime, that man made small by
    his brother's oppression, got stuck forging a helmet with
    magic
enough to make the wearer invisible or, at least, to change his
    shape. Surely, Mime, powerless, himself, to make the
    helmet work on his behalf
did not want his brother, Alberich, to disappear. You can be
    certain the one wanted to get rid of the other, but there
    would likely be more brotherly
reproach, in any case, in making the laughing oppressor think
    himself evaporated when he only stood there, plain,
    beneath the hat, as Mime himself
had stood there, too. That Mime got his kicks, though, anyway.
    While Alberich did really disappear, the gods tricked him
    into something spectacular: that dragon
bent into a toad. We had no idea how any of this was managed
    on stage, say, if there were special effects to make Alberich
    invisible, as his voice

still boomed on stage, or how he might then reappear, a
    greater or lesser amphibian. How it panned out, who
    knows?
The percussion and the voices there were enough to insist
    upon the material nature of it all.

After Wednesday night's production of *Die Walküre*, a critic
    from *The New York Times* said that the scene of immolation
    where
the Wotan understudy (the original pulled out, laryngitic),
    strong enough in his stance against incest to break his own
    domestic solitude, struck the rock
and placed Brünnhilde in a circle of flame, that scene differed
    from Wagner's vision in that those who played the
    Rhinemaidens or the Valkyries or whoever those
figures were, I have forgotten, could be glimpsed circling the
    stage and surrounding Wotan and the goddess as he threw
    her into sleep,
or womanhood. They would not have been on Wagner's stage,
    those girls, the critic said. The scene was only meant for
    two.
Though he conceded this was a matter of taste. Perhaps the
    additional figures, after all, were meant by the director,
Egoyan, to impress upon the audience the isolation of those
    two gods, and to ensure the gravity of their losses.
Perhaps if we had been there, too, and seen it for ourselves, we
    would have better understood.
Though, for us, there had only ever been the two gods singing
    loneliness and all their woe.

Between the acts of Friday afternoon's *Siegfried*, a woman from
    the news was sent to scrutinize the new lounges
and to gauge the reactions of the audience on the third floor of

the house. After interviewing a lady in an evening gown,
the reporter spoke to a man identifying himself as a museum
employee. He was still dressed in his casual uniform,
having run from work, he said, to make it before the curtain.
That man rejoiced in telling the reporter (she had just
been listening to the performance, too, from the speakers in
the lounge) how the dragon whose deep bass we had so
recently enjoyed
appeared on stage surrounded by a pile of humans, a veritable
pyramid of people, he said. In the tone of her reply,
the reporter might be said to have keened disappointment. I
would have only wanted to have seen Fafner there, too, in
his basic dragonhood,
his blood, a fire in the neck of the bass, relaying his thoughts
on a certain curse to Siegfried alone, and not the dreaded crew.

If you had looked for us in the house, the Sunday of the
Götterdämmerung, we would have been hard to find. We
kept to ourselves,
in our independent strategies of a Sunday afternoon, a Sunday
spent checking a reference for a dumb footnote on page
three, or making toast
for someone sick in bed, playing at her pillow hills, already
counting the hours until the next, presumably healthier
weekend,
or bearing up against the winter by binding an old sock or
piling wood in the cellar. The opera, that day, was not with
us for long. Though, near the end, you
could say, we found this kind of bold. At a point, the music just
required a shift in attitude. And a certain elegance associ-
ated with that age
before the advent of the television assumed us there, as we sat
up straight, though not around a family radio, but each of

us, in secret,
with his or her own portable box, or with earbuds and a cozy.
   We would all admit, and readily, that for a moment there,
   we were kept from our piling,
our work, and our play. For a moment, we were all withheld by
   the transmission of Brünnhilde's final breath; for each of us,
alone, she was alone. Though there was something in the sky,
   we said, that lit up with her, too, and broke in through the
   window blinds, and sundered what we knew.

THE EVENING OF YOUR PROPOSAL

That dream was memorable. I was alone in a public park,
raising my hurricane lantern to illuminate the place.
As I travelled among them there, the lovers,
no one moved towards me or my light. I saw them
splayed out along the benches that defined the limits
of the park, couple on couple, each couple
quilted together, their arms like tree roots
struggling in the ground, in secret.

Yes, the park was full of lovers, *plein*.

One man appeared so intense in his task of thrilling
his girl, he kept his eyes open to capture the effects
of his kisses' forward motion in her shoulders'
flitting, as if he had broken a nerve in her. Even his,
those open eyes never motioned towards me, no red glints
caught or returning the expositive light I set about,
those shifts of yellow which seemed with him and among
the others there no exposure after all. No one was moved.

The drunks, as I approached, just kept pissing on

their chosen graffiti beneath the bridges and near
the entrance to the museum. The typical night creatures
set about their typical professions. The bats assembled
from their houses in extraordinary numbers, crevassing
through the air, their senses assured of the deepest cover.
The owls in their trees did not stop feasting on stockpiles
of unlucky mice, bones and all. The restless spiders wove
to outpace the morning dew that might reveal

their targets. And though those targets glistened

slightly in my own lantern's reaching, the spiders
never withdrew. In this light, I could say I caught
everyone without their letting go. I knew then
this was mine, too. I was sure of it. Not there,
in the park, but outside of the dream, and not mine
alone, this consistency which could not be called
oblivion despite its appearance so. This was our own
peace, the willingness and willfulness of our engagement.

THE RESTORATION OF THE IVORY-BILLED WOODPECKER

I.

How many people fail each day, refuse
to heed the warnings set out for us by officials
or conservators or official conservators:
Do not feed the animals, stay on the path,
no recording devices allowed. Like that day
in the Art Gallery of Ontario, when we all turned
to look at one of your favourite paintings,
The Mass of Saint Gregory, the one in which
Jesus rises from the coffin-shaped altar just
as a priest celebrates the transubstantiation.
Neither the priest nor his altar boy appear
surprised at his rising or notice that something once
called miraculous seems to be taking place again
and in their own line of vision. The boy holds
rather than tugs at the priest's vestments. The mass
for them is just another dull event – not much of a rise
for us, either, what with our conversation centred
around the cock and the other souvenirs of the passion
painted to hang there on the wall of Saint Gregory's
church. What appealed to us most was not the body
but the crown of thorns, the rooster, and a thick nail.

So thick, that woman murmured, from her place
across the room, as if to me, *it is so thick and red*.
And she raised her hand and tried it, pointing her finger
upward and over that larger, more fabulous piece:
The Expulsion of the Money-Changers by the Master
of the Kress Epiphany. It was probably only by chance
that I turned to catch a glimpse of her there, rubbing
her index finger hard and slow over one of the red,
lozenge-shaped stones strewn about the temple

on that holy day for barterers. Great works, the most
ambitious accomplishments, it seems, are always
accompanied by the sternest warnings, directives
to limit our touch, our access to, and hence
our experience of things, polite requests and firmer
imperatives which stymie our pleasures and desires,
even if we have only brought ourselves there,
in the face of those magnetic objects, those
certifiable masterpieces of nature and art, to justify
another person's notions after all. Just then I found
myself, observed myself, really, (no one finds themselves
these days) indignant and curatorial. I stood there,
with my mouth agape, afraid for the life of the painting
and stunned by that woman's gall.

                              So then,
I stood apart from you all, wondering how
her abuse might multiply. What would happen
to that glossy, painted stone if it were rubbed
a thousand times by the same or similar hands,
hands like hers or mine, rubbed impatiently out
of some brief fascination, or soberly, and with love?
That stone might seem to vanish, almost, entirely,
until the Kress's painted Jesus (livelier than our own),
baffled by what was happening in and around the temple,
appeared to be beating the moneylenders, toppling
their tables of trade goods and sending them out
of the temple with far less reason than he ought, or,
in some stunning reversal, with more reason than
we ever thought possible. That Jesus might have stood
swinging and swatting at the moneylenders, there,
surrounded by lovely, luminous, rubbed-out lozenges
heaved into the air, money-lozenges that in their faded state

looked like what we might have imagined, at least,
in the context of that newer draft, to be souls rising.
It was only natural, then, that as I moved to raise
my voice and in my voice's failing to tell her to *stop
touching that painting*, that it was *against the rules*,
I wanted to be that woman there, rubbing the chits.
It was only natural that having seen that woman
standing there with her hand pursed just so, I wanted
to put my own finger on that thick, red piece, that jewel,
before it vanished, or in order to vanish it into soul.

II.

As children, my brother and I, we lived along
what was once a rural route in Forsythe County,
Georgia. A few times a year, the school there
sat us down for a lesson in biology, showing us each
and every time, the same filmstrip they had shown
for years: *The Disappearance of the Ivory-Billed
Woodpecker*. I suppose the film made it easier for them,
our teachers, to express something about nature
and ecology without directly tackling evolution or sex-
education. Those black and white stills of the bird in flight,
the first and last footage ever to be recorded of the creature
that had since, as far as the man on the voice-over tape
was concerned, made itself extinct, or abstained
at least from human contact, for all it is worth, keeping
so far out of eye and earshot that no one could claim
to have seen it, anyway (extinction, after all, is difficult,
if not impossible to prove – you would have to scour
the earth with an impeccable eye and be absolutely sure
you had not simply missed what you were looking for),
no matter how many times we saw that film, that bird
flitting from the screen, or were told by the regretful voice
on the taped commentary that the bird and his entire
species were likely vanished for good, rubbed out
from even the wildest of places, that filmstrip always got
us going. We would rush (you would have, too)
with our friends from the neighbourhood out into our back-
yards, those woods which extended into other woods
which at the time belonged to no one, calling for that bird
and listening for his ancient response. We would hunt
in groups or delve secretly, in our own private hours,
in case that impossible bird, with his impossible tap

and his impossibly white bill might reveal himself to us
alone. I am sure it made a real scientist out of at least
one of us, that mass of fancy the filmstrip stirred up,
substituting for lessons and textbooks and our teachers'
demure drawls. Of the rest of us, at least, it made temporary
explorers, shook us out of our habits into a new kind
of restlessness. In the days that followed we would turn
up in class with the exoskeletons of insects we had found
clinging to the trees, claiming that at least a few of them,
rather than escaping from their first skins into the heavy
weather, a few of those bugs must have been taken
by the woodpecker in his secret predations. Our teachers,
then, were satisfied. We had come to an understanding.

III.

A moment of astonishment from the free paper
in the market last Tuesday (newspapers, too,
they say, may one day become extinct): *Plucked
from Extinction, the Ivory-Billed Woodpecker* is no
longer considered vanished. One lone, giant male
was spotted amidst an expanse of forest in Arkansas –
the newest jar. At some point in the last few weeks
a man with a video camera caught the elusive bird alive,
at rest, and then in motion, nailed him, we are told,
on film, and with no harm done to the thing itself.
The media, at least the Tuesday paper media, went reeling
over the improbability of such a find, portioning out
in no subtle proportions the epic consequence
of the discovery itself, though this discovery, too,
in the context of the reports, seemed like any one
of our present-day rages. *This is huge . . . It's kind
of like finding Elvis*, they went, some waxing poetical
as they watched *a winged ghost . . . flitting about the tupelo
trees in the Big Woods of Arkansas*, allowing
for an extra dash of wonder in this their daily grace.
But that bird was not once a ghost, and what with
the initial discovery broken, there would be more work
in the warning than in the wondering after all.

Even in that breaking Tuesday morning report,
the media anticipated the rage that might follow
upon the initial vision, the money shot, when all
the scientists and birdwatchers set out for a closer look,
when those of us who recall the earlier footage,
remembering our own bouts of exploration, started
making plans to go and see it for ourselves, or when

even just the normals, reading the story for the first time
felt a twinge of something sacred stirring within
and struck out to find the woodpecker, too, that bird
caught still and in our own century by that videographer
what's-his-name. And so the paper's imperatives
got set down in fast running print to foil us all, the birders,
those who grew up along the film strip circuit, and
the normals alike, to keep us all from running down
to that hollow in God's country with our cameras
or even just with our raw eyes for a glimpse of the thing.
Do not follow it. One man's capture is enough.

It makes sense, I suppose, for us all to *refrain from going out*
to some spot in the woods in Arkansas and scaring that bird
half to death, trampling its nest or the precious ground
below. To stand in the general vicinity of where that bird
might one day procreate with the still hidden female,
her wings reddening, his body stiff as stone, the both
of them re-emerging from the thick with an entire species
once thought vanished, for good, that would be criminal.
No good looking as they store and warm their eggs. No good
chasing after the good old bird that has already made
itself known. No. *The paths would grow so dull, the woods
so extensively damaged*, it is no wonder, though it is thorny,
though it stings for a few minutes or maybe a little longer, say,
if it bears upon your own story, if you have been in the know,
no wonder they keep telling us *not to go into the woods now*,
and not to drive into extinction this wingèd that never left.

DAUGHTER AND SON

We planted a self-fruiting cherry tree beside the obelisk
crowned with honeysuckle. It all appears exotic.
The leaves of the tree, thin as an infant's fingers,
and the tree's thinner branches thicken in the breeze.
The honeysuckle's yellow tips and teardrops fly
the wooden stand. The young and younger planted there
together form the kind of lean tableau you would likely find
as a line drawing in a nineteen-seventies *Bible*. That tree
and obelisk might very well glance over the famed waters
of Babylon or stand towards the back in that scene where
the whore appears the only one to bother bringing well-
water to the traveller. The other women there, we read,
had already completed their business and left.

It is likely the honeysuckle will come back next year.
Though, it is of little consequence. Who knows how long
this particular cherry tree will last either, though we do
our best to encourage the roots. Even if it survives,
who knows if it will ever come to flower. The raccoons
and the sparrows living here will likely steal the cherries,
anyway, before we step across the lawn to do the gathering.
It is of no matter. It is immaterial. Just looking at them there,
like that, you know that you will always have your fruit.

EPILOGUE

CURSES

Do not be surprised if, having been asked to perform
some service or ceremony, and flying from it, you
have your turn with curses. You pass a dead squirrel
or a pigeon, maybe, and you fail to place it in a bag
or to call the city to see if it might require additional
inspection by those schooled in disease. There will be
consequences for flying this or any other scene. You
might lose your voice in the time designated for singing,
or you might not recover just as quickly as you thought
from one of your more somber attitudes. Some day,
that dead body, as if alive and breathing, or its double
of a slightly different hue, might very well call you out
with its less-than-appealing lung-shot and give you the tumble
you have long been wanting, not just turning you off the path,
or dirtying your suit, but nice damage, concussing,
or even hollowing out your more mysterious eye.
At this point, it will be too late to return to the place
where you failed to perform your service. Why take
the chance that your own particular comeuppance
will be the lesser of these griefs, when you might spare
yourself entirely, by crossing yourself as you should,
whistling a brief requiem for the little vermin, or cursing
the sportsman or the gas company or the god who surely
planned this body's fall from the tree beside your house?
This figure which stands for the last of its species, as any dead
body would, why not just take care of it at first with a tent-
fold of the morning news and a liberal fist of dirt?

NOTES

"To a Translator of Horace": The speaker refers to David Ferry's *The Odes of Horace* (Farrar, Straus, and Giroux, 1998), particularly i.28, "A Beach Near Tarentum." Some references to the latter lines of this poem are also made in "Curses." As reported in Anne McIlroy's "Going to Extremes to Fight Global Warming," Edward Teller, father of the hydrogen bomb, was "one of the most prominent early proponents of using geoengineering to fight global warming," *The Globe and Mail*, (Toronto), June 3, 2006.

"Surveillance": The epigraph is taken from Emily Dickinson's poem #1233. *Kudzu* is an Eastern Asian vine imported into the American South by mistake. It grows over natural and unnatural objects in sheets like a tarpaulin or dust cover.

"Miners' Houses": This poem references Lawren S. Harris' *Miners' Houses, Glace Bay*, 1925. Art Gallery of Ontario.

"The Ears of Kings": The garden referred to here is on the campus of Northwestern University (Evanston, Illinois). Eugene Schieffelin, head of the American Acclimatization Society for European Settlers, released approximately eighty European Starlings (*Sturnus vulgaris*) in New York's Central Park in March of 1890 and forty more the following year.

"The End of the Novel": Loose models for the speaker here are Stephen Marche's *Raymond and Hannah*, Ian MacEwen's *Atonement,* and Iris Murdoch's *The Sea, The Sea*.

"A Muscle in the Country": The final lines refer to Robert Frost's "The Need of Being Versed in Country Things."

"Annotations on your Pastoral, *Summer*": The speaker responds to Alexis in "Summer" from Alexander Pope's *Pastorals*.

"Of Minor Figures": The Old English quotation from Ælfric's *Life of St. Edmund* has been set into verse by Robin J. Norris. The translation which follows is the poet's.

"Notes on Immigration": For "the professor my husband writes about," see "At the Offices of the Perishable Press" by Blaise Moritz from *Crown and Ribs* (Fitzhenry and Whiteside, 2007). The lines on the mynah are inspired by Wayne Grady's *Bringing Back the Dodo* (McClelland & Stewart, 2006).

"The Course of the Renovations, I": For the past few years, as Transformation AGO has been underway, the museum has offered only a limited selection of its permanent collection for public viewing. "The Thomson gifts" are the 2,000 works of art donated to the museum from the private collection of Mr. Kenneth Thomson, the largest gift made from a private donor to a Canadian cultural institution. The final painting referenced is Frederick H. Varley's *Dharana*, c.1932.

"The Course of the Renovations, II": The extension to the Royal Ontario Museum is known as The Crystal, and the initiative, Renaissance ROM.

"A Newer Wilderness": The speaker refers to Ray Bradbury's "A Sound of Thunder."

"During the Spring Dandelion Rush in Irvine, California": This piece incorporates and transforms lines from the closure of *Book One* of William Cowper's *The Task*, lines 749-774, beginning, "God made the country, and man made the town."

"A Child's Garden" references Robert Frost's "A Girl's Garden."

"Lazarus Speaks in Front of Lemieux's *Lazare*, 1941": i.e. Jean-Paul Lemieux, *Lazare*, 1941. Art Gallery of Ontario.

"A Newer Wilderness (II)": The speaker responds to a book review of Dennis Lee's *UN*. "UN: An Uncanny Unraveling," Karen Solie, *The Globe and Mail*, (Toronto), April 12, 2003.

"The Masters of the Country House Poems": This poem incorporates and transforms lines from poems considered part of or critical of the Country House tradition outlined by Raymond Williams in *The Country and the City*. Some of these are: William Shakespeare, *Macbeth* I.vi., Thomas Carew, "To Saxham," Robert Herrick, "A Panegerick to Sir Lewis Pemberton," Charles Cotton, "A Journey into the Peak: To Sir Aston Cokayne," Ben Jonson, "To Penshurst," Andrew Marvell, "Upon Appleton House," and Derek Walcott, "The Star-Apple Kingdom."

"Opera Week in Radio": On September 12, 2006, the Four Seasons Centre for the Performing Arts opened with a performance of Wagner's *Das Rheingold*. The Canadian Opera Company, under the direction of Richard Bradshaw, presented the entire cycle, *Der Ring des Nibelungen*, over the course of the week. Howard Dick hosted the complete coverage of the series on CBC Radio Two. Atom Egoyan is the director mentioned by last name in the second stanza.

"The Restoration of the Ivory-Billed Woodpecker": At some point in the late 1990's at the Art Gallery of Ontario, Simon Marmion's *The Mass of Saint Gregory*, ca.1460–65, hung in a gallery opposite the Master of the Kress Epiphany's *The Expulsion of the Money-Changers*, ca. 1480-1490. Some of the italicized phrases are from "Plucked from Extinction; 60 Years Since Ivory-billed Specimen Seen, Birders Expected to Descend on Arkansas Forests," Megan Ogilvie, *Toronto Star*, April 29, 2005. There are also echoes here of the title poem of Susan Stewart's *The Forest*, (University of Chicago Press, 1995).

ACKNOWLEDGEMENTS

The sequence *Kenotaphion* appeared in its entirety in the *Malahat Review* 143 (2003) as co-winner of the journal's biennial long poem prize. "During the Spring Dandelion Rush in Irvine, California" and "Surveillance" also appeared in the *Malahat Review* 137 (2001), the former being nominated for a National Magazine Award in Canada.

"The Wife of Pilate" and "Certain Disappearances" appeared in *The Fiddlehead* 215 (2002).

"Surveillance" and "During the Spring Dandelion Rush in Irvine, California" were also published as an artist's book, entitled *A Newer Wilderness* which featured original linocuts by Blaise Moritz (Urban Farm and Philomel Dada, 2000).

"Surveillance," "Certain Disappearances," "The Wife of Pilate," "During the Spring Dandelion Rush in Irvine, California," and "A Newer Wilderness" appeared in a small-press chapbook, also entitled *A Newer Wilderness* (Philomel Dada, 2002).

Thanks to the Toronto Arts Council and to the Canada Council for the Arts for generous support of this project.

Thanks to Paul Vermeersch, Mike O'Connor, Dan Varrette, Gillian Urbankiewicz, and Alysia Shewchuk for preparing and presenting this work to the public.

And thanks, as ever, to my husband Blaise, and to our children. "For nought but Love / can answer Love, and render Bliss secure." – Thomson